By Joy Cowley

Illustrated by E. Silas Smith

Dominie Press, Inc.

Publisher: Christine Yuen
Editor: John S. F. Graham
Designer: Lois Stanfield
Illustrator: E. Silas Smith

Text Copyright © 2002 Joy Cowley
Illustrations Copyright © 2002 Dominie Press, Inc.
All rights reserved. No part of this publication may be reproduced or transmitted in any form or by any means without permission in writing from the publisher. Reproduction of any part of this book, through photocopy, recording, or any electronic or mechanical retrieval system, without the written permission of the publisher, is an infringement of the copyright law.

Published by:
Dominie Press, Inc.
1949 Kellogg Avenue
Carlsbad, California 92008 USA

www.dominie.com

Paperback ISBN 0-7685-1090-2
Library Bound Edition ISBN 0-7685-1528-9
Printed in Singapore by PH Productions Pte Ltd
  2 3 4 5 6 PH 04

Table of Contents

Chapter One
Dangerous Cargo 4

Chapter Two
Captain Mom 9

Chapter Three
Asteroids .13

Chapter Four
Seven-Inch Gap 21

Chapter Five
Emergency! 30

Chapter One
Dangerous Cargo

It was a long journey back home to Mars. *The Phoebus* towed an ore wagon that was loaded with flash rock from Chiron, and it was dangerous cargo. Conrad was the first child ever to travel with a load of flash rock. He was on the ship because his mother was the captain.

Conrad heard Officer Zeej talking about it. "It's not right to have a kid with us. I tell you, it's very bad luck!"

Mr. Jefferson, the engineer, laughed. "Come on, Zeej. You don't really think that.

What was the boy going to do? Stay on his own on Mars for eight months?"

"She should have found someone to look after him," growled Officer Zeej.

"Have a heart," said Mr. Jefferson. "Conrad's all she's got. She needs him. He needs her. It's just the two of them. You know that."

"That's no reason why we should put ourselves in danger," Officer Zeej insisted. "To take a child on a voyage like this means disaster for everyone."

Mr. Jefferson laughed again. "Ah, Zeej! You and your old Martian superstitions! Come on! I challenge you to a game of anti-gravity chess."

After they had gone to the games room, Conrad lay on his bunk, thinking. At least he found out why Officer Zeej didn't like him. It was nothing personal, just a superstition. Why were kids supposed to bring bad luck? He didn't know. Maybe it was because they got in the way if something went wrong.

Conrad knew that flash rock was the most dangerous ore in the universe. It was very unstable. It had to be kept at the right temperature. If it became too warm or too cold, it lived up to its name. You could explode in one huge flash.

His mother, Captain Edna, told him there was nothing to worry about. "Sure, flash rock can kill. But it can also give life. We need it to make oxygen on Mars. These ore wagons are designed to keep it at exactly the right temperature. The main computer system sees to that."

"But what if the computer fails?" he asked.

"There's a secondary system, Conrad," she said. "It takes over."

"And if that fails?"

"We can adjust the temperature manually." She ruffled his hair. "But nothing is going to fail, Conrad. These ships are very reliable. Now, go and do your schoolwork."

Chapter Two
Captain Mom

That was the worst thing about the captain being your mother. You had to do what you were told. Conrad wanted to spend more time on the bridge. The wonder of space filled him with excitement. When he looked out at distant suns and nebulas, his heart beat faster. He felt like an explorer inside a huge body. The galaxies were like living cells. The ship was a microbe, traveling inside a huge creature called *the universe.*

The other exciting place was the games room. In there, you could switch gravity on or off. You could play regular basketball, or you could play anti-gravity basketball. You could shoot from above the hoops, not knowing which way the ball would go.

But when your mother was the captain, you spent most of your time with schoolwork.

Conrad liked astro-mapping. His new hologram computer told him when he put a planet in the wrong place. But he wasn't so wild about the old Earth languages. His mother was making him learn Spanish, French, and Japanese.

"Why?" he asked her. "Nobody on Mars ever uses old Earth languages."

"They're the history of your people," his mother said. "You don't know a planet's history until you've learned its languages. Next

you'll do Russian, Italian, and Mandarin."

"Do I have to?" he groaned.

His mother laughed. "Why are you complaining? In the old days, people had to learn languages the hard way. All you have to do is wear your language headsets. The words go directly into your brain."

"Yeah, yeah, yeah," he said.

"What was that?" she said.

Conrad stood up straight and saluted. "Yes, Captain Mom!"

"Much better," she said, turning to leave.

Conrad grinned. "Excuse me, Captain Mom?"

"Yes?" She stopped.

"When I've finished, can I please play space pirates?"

His mother smiled. "Sure," she said.

Chapter Three

Asteroids

Conrad was in the middle of his Spanish lesson when the emergency light came on. It flashed red on the wall by his bunk, like an angry heartbeat. He sat up, taking off his Spanish headset.

What was happening?

Officer Ching put her head in the doorway. "The captain sent me, Conrad. She said not to worry. It's just an asteroid warning."

"We're going to go through an asteroid belt?" he asked.

"No, we'll go around it. But we might see it in the distance. Have you ever seen an asteroid belt before?"

He shook his head. "Never."

"Then come on up to the bridge." She waved her hand.

Conrad looked at his headset. "What about my lessons?"

Officer Ching smiled. "Your Mom says this is part of your education, too. But if you want to stay here…"

"No, no!" He was off his bunk in an instant. "I want to see the asteroids."

He followed Officer Ching the length of the ship. But when he stepped onto the bridge, he heard an angry yell from Officer Zeej. "What is that kid doing here?"

Conrad blinked. There were five people on

the bridge, including Mr. Jefferson and Officer Zeej. Officer Zeej and the captain were standing by the navigation screen. Officer Zeej looked angry.

"It's all right, Zeej," said the captain. "I sent for him."

"No!" cried Officer Zeej. "This is the worst time. This is..."

"I said it's all right," the captain said firmly. "Conrad, take that seat and buckle yourself in. Don't be alarmed. We're just being careful. The asteroid belt is much bigger than we thought. With a full load of flash rock, we couldn't move fast enough to avoid it. This ship is as strong as a mountain. But it'll be a bumpy ride."

"He shouldn't be here," muttered Officer Zeej.

Conrad's mother wasn't listening. She was busy setting the new course and giving orders to the crew.

Conrad knew how to fasten the safety harness. He'd done it for every takeoff. He lay back in his seat. When he turned his head, he could see outside. The sky was empty. Not an asteroid in sight.

His mother was by the navigation screen. He heard her say, "The change in course means we'll miss most of it. The problem area is here. It'll feel like a ten-second earthquake."

Earthquake? Conrad had never been on Earth. But he had seen old films of shaking buildings. This, he thought, was going to be exciting.

The sky was dark and quiet.

"All right," said Captain Edna. "Everyone brace for impact."

All around Conrad there was a click of seat buckles. After that, no one moved. No one spoke. The ship hummed as though it was singing to itself. Everything was so still, Conrad thought maybe his mother was wrong. Maybe they had completely missed the asteroids. Maybe it was all a big nothing.

Wham!

He didn't see the first one, but he felt it. The ship lurched. *Wham!* The jolt was in his chair and in his bones. He gasped. There was still nothing to be seen out there. *Wham! Wham!* His teeth rattled. There was only a dark blur.

Wham! Wham! Wham!

He had expected to see rocks coming

toward them. But there was just a rushing blackness and then the terrible noises. Crashing sounds! Screaming metal! The straps tightened around his chest, and he couldn't breathe. It was like a Martian ice storm. He was being tossed around, this way, that way. *Bash! Bash! Screech!*

The lights on the bridge flickered. He heard a sizzle of sparks. He smelled smoke.

Then it went quiet and dark.

Chapter Four
Seven-Inch Gap

Conrad stayed in his seat while the crew used their emergency lights to check the damage to *The Phoebus*.

"Main system is out," said Mr. Jefferson.

"Okay," said Captain Edna in her calm voice. "That means we need time for repairs. Switch on the secondary system."

Conrad turned his head as far as he could. He could see shadowy shapes moving fast, flipping switches, punching in computer codes.

A green light filled the bridge, and there was a faint whirring noise.

"Sixty percent damage to the secondary system," said Mr. Jefferson. "We don't have enough power to stabilize the temperature in the ore wagon."

There was a short silence. Captain Edna said, still using her calm voice, "Well, thank goodness the designer of this ship didn't put all his trust in computers. Jefferson, you need to go into the ore wagon and operate the manual system."

"I'm on it," said Mr. Jefferson. "Ching, what's the temperature back there?"

Officer Ching looked at her screen. "Gone up three degrees," she said.

"I'll put on my running shoes," said Mr. Jefferson with a forced laugh.

Conrad wanted to talk to his mother, but she was busy. She gave orders in a normal

voice, but he could tell she was worried. She always frowned when things went wrong.

Mr. Jefferson came back, out of breath. "We've had a major hit on the linkage," he gasped.

Conrad looked quickly at his mother. He saw her frown deepen. The linkage was the narrow passageway between the ship and the ore wagon full of flash rock.

"The door's jammed," said Mr. Jefferson. "It's open about seven inches. It won't go any wider."

"Are you sure?" Captain Edna asked.

"Absolutely," Mr. Jefferson said. "It's so damaged, there's nowhere for the door to slide to."

"I see." The captain took a deep breath and let it out again. "Ching, how's the temperature?"

"Up four degrees and rising," replied Officer Ching.

The captain slowly shook her head. "We have no choice," she said. "We have to jettison the ore wagon."

Conrad felt the defeat in her voice. Now they would have to let the wagon go. It was a big container, shaped like the abdomen of an insect. It would drift for a while in space. Then it would explode, a quick, bright flash in the darkness. A valuable cargo would be gone, and eight months' work would be wasted. It was a terrible thing to happen to his mother.

Conrad undid his safety harness, jumped down from his seat, and ran toward her. Officer Zeej pushed him away. "See what you've done, boy?" he snapped.

Captain Edna was too busy to notice.

"Stand by to jettison ore wagon," she said. "Five, four, three, two, one. Release!" She pulled a lever.

Nothing happened.

She pulled it again. She rattled it as though she was trying to shake the ore wagon loose. Still nothing happened.

"It's not just the door," said Mr. Jefferson in a quiet voice. "The asteroids have damaged the breakaway system."

Captain Edna tried the lever once more. Then she said, "How long before we get full power back?"

"Five hours," said Officer Zeej.

"How long before the rock reaches flash temperature?" she asked.

"About thirty minutes," replied Officer Ching.

Conrad felt his mouth go dry. They were stuck with a load of flash rock that was getting hotter and more unstable by the minute. In half an hour it would explode.

His mother clenched her fists. "This is so frustrating! We've got manual control in the wagon, and no one can reach it. Jefferson, can you try the door again?"

Mr. Jefferson shook his head. "It won't budge."

"Can't you cut through the door?" said Officer Zeej.

"We could if we had full power," Mr. Jefferson replied.

Conrad measured seven inches with his hands. It was a very small gap, but he was kind of skinny. "I think I could get through," he said.

"No!" cried his mother.

"Temperature up six degrees and rising," said Officer Ching.

Mr. Jefferson looked at Conrad. "He might just get in there."

Captain Edna shook her head. "Definitely not!"

"Please, Mom!" Conrad begged. "Let me try!"

"I hate to spell this out," said Mr. Jefferson. "But this boy might be our only chance."

Chapter Five

Emergency!

Back home on Mars, Conrad's mom sometimes made crust for pies. She let him flatten it with something she called a *rolling pin*. As Conrad squeezed through the narrow gap, he thought he might come out as thin as pie crust.

He rubbed his bruised chest. "I'm in," he called to Mr. Jefferson.

Mr. Jefferson handed him a radio and a flashlight through the gap.

"Good boy," he said. "When you get to the control panel, I'll tell you what to do."

"Yes, sir." Conrad attached the radio to his shirt. He aimed his light into the ore wagon, which was like a giant supermarket with floor-to-ceiling shelves. The only thing stored on those shelves was flash rock. The beam from his light passed over thousands of steel crates packed with the stuff. Right now, it looked harmless enough. But the air in the wagon was warm and getting warmer.

His footsteps clanged on steel grating. Spooky shadows moved around his light.

"Are you there yet?" asked Mr. Jefferson through the radio.

"Nearly, sir. Yes, yes, here it is." He turned the light to a panel of controls set in the wall. "What now?"

"The buttons in the middle row are the

temperature controls. There are four of them. Got that?"

Conrad held his light closer. "Yes, sir. I can see them."

"Begin at the left," crackled the radio. "Press the first key, then count to five. Press the second key. Count to five. Do the same for the third and fourth. Start now."

Conrad pushed his finger against the first square button. It clicked down and he counted: *one, two, three, four, five.* He pushed the button next to it and counted again.

The air in the wagon was getting warmer, and it had a sharp smell. Conrad coughed. Flash rock let off fumes when it was getting unstable.

He pushed the fourth button. "Done that,

sir," he said. "Sir, the flash rock is starting to smell."

"I know," said Mr. Jefferson. "I can smell it from here. Okay, you've set up the manual system. Now all you have to do is open the vents. Turn the big wheel clockwise."

Conrad put his hand on the wheel and tried to turn it. It didn't move. He tried again. He put the flashlight between his teeth and grabbed the wheel with both hands. It wouldn't move an inch.

The sharp smell of flash rock made him cough again. His flashlight fell to the floor and he doubled over, his hands over his mouth.

"Are you all right?" came Mr. Jefferson's voice over the radio.

Conrad gasped, "No, sir. It—it won't turn. It's stuck."

"Hit it with something!" Mr. Jefferson cried.

Conrad looked at his flashlight. It was made of plastic. "With what?"

"Listen, Conrad! The cargo's on red alert. You have to work fast. There should be a toolkit in there. Grab something. Loosen that wheel or—" The radio crackled loudly.

A new voice came on. "Conrad, do you hear me?" It was his mother. "Get out of there right now! We've got a little more power. We're going to try to release the ore wagon."

Conrad coughed and pointed his flashlight around the shelves of flash rock. The air was misty with fumes, and he couldn't see all that well.

"Conrad?" His mother's voice was urgent. "Get out of there!"

He couldn't stop coughing. His light jerked over the shelves, and then the floor. Suddenly, he saw a metal ore shovel. It was square with a long handle. It was used to scrape small pieces of rock off the grating.

"Conrad?" Now his mother was yelling. "Out! Out!"

He didn't have time to talk. He dragged the shovel over to the control panel. He knew hitting the wheel wouldn't work, but he could use the handle as a lever.

"Conrad!" the radio screamed.

He dropped his flashlight to the floor. Then he slid the handle of the shovel through the wheel and wedged the shovel blade in the floor grating. He pushed down on the handle with all the strength he had.

The wheel turned.

A blast of cold air hit him in the face. He

let the shovel drop and turned the wheel the rest of the way by hand. The wagon filled with a roaring sound. The gust of air made his shirt flap against his chest. The deadly mist was gone. His eyes were still itchy and watering from the fumes, but now he could take a deep, clean breath. He picked up his flashlight and headed for the linkage, still coughing.

He squeezed through the seven-inch gap to get back to the ship. He didn't know how many people were waiting for him at the linkage door. He still couldn't see very well, but he heard cheering and felt people hugging him. It sounded like a party.

He heard Mr. Jefferson yell, "Temperature's down three degrees already!" and his mother was saying, "Oh Conrad! Conrad!"

He was cold and tired. He still felt like pie crust. But that didn't matter too much. He had done his job, and he felt good.

Then he heard another voice. It was Officer Zeej shouting, "The kid has saved the ship! He has saved us all!"